God Made Me Black Because He is Creative © 2020 by Julie K. Federico.

All rights reserved. No part of this publication may be reproduced, stored in a retrieval system, or transmitted in any way by any means, electronic, mechanical, photocopy, recording, or otherwise without the prior permission of the author except as provided by USA copyright law.

Published by Julie Federico

Children's Services Author. www.juliefederico.com

All rights reserved. Cover design & Interior design by Emma Smith at Vox Illustration.

Creative title of this book created by Keita Andrews

Published in the United States of America

ISBN: 978-1-63760-777-0

God made some people black, some white, some a shade of red, and others caramel. There are lots of different shades in humanity! This is exciting because every thing is not the same. There are differences in human skin tone. This is part of God's wonderfully creative plan, this is intentional.

You can also see his creativity in nature. There are so many kinds of flowers, it is hard to identify them all. Each night the sunset looks different, which also shows a part of God's creative side. He never runs out of ideas; he never makes mistakes. After all these centuries, he is still glad he made people different colors on the color chart.

Because of unfair rules and practices set by society, government, schools, police departments, and the court system, black people and other people of color have been and are currently being mistreated. This is called discrimination. Black and brown people have been and are currently being mistreated just because of the color of their skin. This is always wrong.

Discrimination needs to stop today, right now. Children can help bring about this change by the things they do and say. You can help end discrimination today! You can do this by treating everyone you meet with respect: Open doors for other people when their hands are full; ask other kids who may be a different color than you to play at recess; or even better, ask them over to your house after school to play or study. Make lasting friendships with kids who are a different color than you. All of these acts will help to end discrimination.

We are all the same on the inside, even though our skin colors may be different. Certain people should not have a life of privilege while others receive mistreatment just because of the color of their skin. This needs to change in our society.

Remember, the only reason our outsides look different is that God created us in a variety of beautiful skin tones. People's skin color is different because of God's creativity not because one race is superior to another. I think children can start to dismantle this problem easier than adults can. As children you have the power to see these problems as solvable, children are not afraid to talk about race issues. Children offer solutions as they see things just as they are, and they do not sugarcoat or dismiss racist behavior. All of these things go a long way when a community is working to end discrimination. There is not one fix for this problem but many.

Children by nature do not discriminate, this is why they are the perfect group to help end discrimination. Adults can learn a lot from children if they will stop and listen. I want to empower all children to break the cycle of discrimination today. There is no greater work to be done. All races matter, everyone is important, everyone deserves the same opportunities and privileges.

I want to encourage you to help end discrimination today and every day. We need more acceptance of all races to make our world a better place! Would you like to join me in this important work? I am so happy you said, "Yes!" Together, we can end racial discrimination and make positive much-needed changes. We need everyone's help to spread kindness and end discrimination. Everyone deserves to live free from discrimination.

Author's NotE

My gifted Pastor at Colorado Community Church Keita Andrews used the title of this book in an impromptu sermon he gave one morning in the summer of 2020. He spoke to a group of volunteers getting ready to clean up graffiti downtown at the State Capital. As soon as he said it I thought, "Oh, this is good!" Fortunately, it did not leave my memory so that you can benefit from this wisdom.

I struggled with the right words for this book, knowing I might encounter criticism for what I did not mention: Police brutality, Breonna Taylor, George Floyd, and institutional incarceration, just to name a few. This was intentional, though. As a child's first book on race relations, I wanted to begin the conversation in an age-appropriate manner. This book will get the conversation started but requires further study as kids get older.

I wrote this book for preschoolers and elementary students. Ideally, you will have many conversations with your child about race over the years. These conversations will change as your child gets older. When we can teach a community of 2-year-olds to identify and define discrimination, we are onto significant societal change! My goal is to introduce the subject and get the conversation started. Young people are not afraid to talk about race. Unlike many adults, they do not possess hesitation and conversation-dodging behaviors. For these reasons, I am excited to share this book with your family and your school. Please continue this important conversation with your children, I am available for author visits. I don't have all of the answers to combat discrimination and generational systemic racism but I am not afraid to talk about it and problem solve.

Julie Federico www.juliefederico.com
August 2020

Teacher's Guide

If you are a teacher reading this drop the word God from the story, it will still be effective.

If you are a teacher and reading this to your class give yourself a huge pat on the back! It is not easy to discuss topics of race. Thank you for being brave enough to do this, you are changing history in your community and beyond by your work. Relax, children do not have the same hang-ups that adults do when discussing these topics. Kids are open, transparent, and ask the most interesting questions. I would love to hear some of them if you have time to email me. Notice your own biases before discussing this book with your class. Just be aware, you do not have to be perfect to do this lesson.

This is a book ideally you would read more than once to your class, it takes time for the details to sink in. Kids' questions will change and become more in-depth as they learn more. When this happens you know you are making a difference.

Define discrimination: Discrimination happens when one group of people treats another group of people poorly just because of their race/color. Real-life activity: I use birthdays instead of one's race because this is less threatening. Have students in two groups: students born from January to June.

Then another group, born from July to December. Choose one group to be discriminated against. Then say to the class, "This group does not have the same opportunities to locate secure employment because of when their birthday is. This group does not get to have the same opportunities when they apply to and attend college.

This group is more likely to have law enforcement called on them for a school-related discipline offense." The kids will rebel and say, "That is not fair, no one gets to pick when they are born. How come it is this way? This will allow for further quality discussion. Ask each of their questions back to the group to see if any students in your class can answer these difficult questions. Then step in with your own thoughts. One question I love to ask kids is, "Now that you know how discrimination is set up what would you do to stop it?" I would have kids make a picture or write an essay on this. I would share the winning essay with your local newspaper.

Communities are looking for answers to this question. I know the local newspaper would love to print it. Kids are extremely creative, they live outside the box that most adults are stuck in. You will be amazed by their answers. As you wrap up the exercise ask the group that was discriminated against how it felt to them and what they thought of being on the wrong end of discrimination. Ask if they could now empathize with groups that are being discriminated against. Ask them if they have seen discrimination up close inside or outside of school. If you have students of color in your classroom listen very closely and empathically to their stories. Say anything except, "Are you sure it happened that way?" This does not validate their reality. Unless you are a person of color their stories will most likely shock you. Kids witness and experience discrimination at very young ages. Let them talk, validate them and learn from their stories. When you do this work a little goes a long way. You do not have to ask every question listed when you do this exercise. Sometimes side conversations will start that are more important than the main one. Lastly, I like to ask students, "What type of discrimination have you seen at our school?" Ultimately you can not change the whole world, but you can change your world and recreate systems/processes that are not working for all families.

Listen carefully to the students' responses, take notes and share them with your Principal. You do not have to have all of the answers, you are just starting this very important conversation. Thank you so much for the work you do!

Other titles by Julie Federico www.juliefederico.com

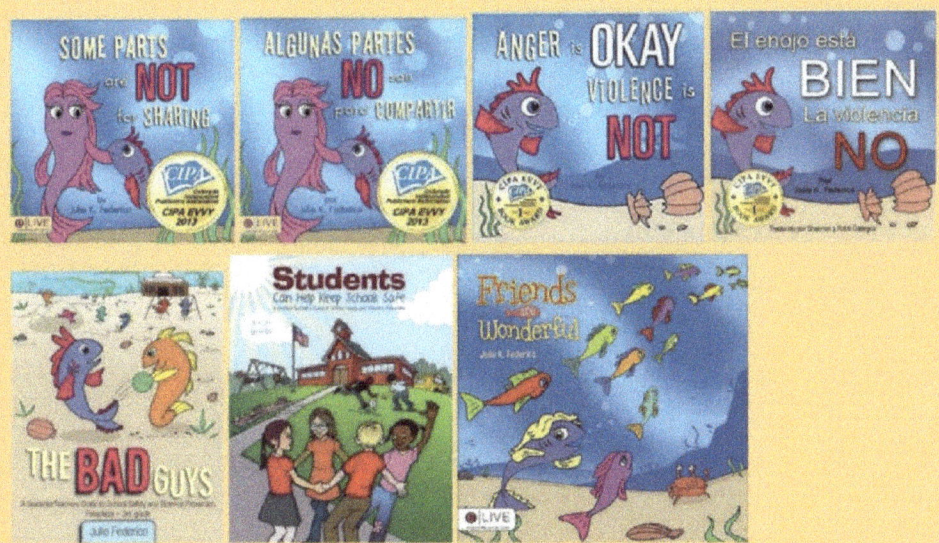

www.ingramcontent.com/pod-product-compliance
Lightning Source LLC
Chambersburg PA
CBHW042033100526
44587CB00029B/4398